The Praying Flute

"Song of the Earth Mother"

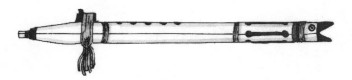

A Bald Mountain Story

written and illustrated
by
Tony Shearer

Library of Congress Cataloging in Publication Data

Shearer, Tony
    The Praying Flute

Cover Painting of Wolf Robe
by Tony Shearer and Deborah Buttrey.

Books for a better world

Naturegraph Publishers, Inc.
P.O. Box 1075
Happy Camp, CA 96039
U.S.A.

Dedicated to
The Uniqueness
and beauty of
Indian People
Everywhere

And Especially
To
Rosalie M. Jones
"Daystar"

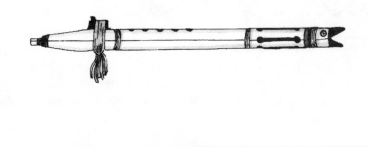

INTRODUCTION

By Rosalie M. Jones, Director of DAYSTAR:
The Theatre of Oral Traditions

It was in the summer of 1981 that I made my first contact with Tony Shearer. It was not face to face, but through the pages of a book called *Lord of the Dawn,* which I purchased at a book store in the Minneapolis airport—on my way coming and going in my travels as a solo dance artist. This time, I was on my way to Ladysmith, Wisconsin, to spend a summer with my master teacher, Barry Lynn. It was that summer that I created "La Malinche: The Story of One Grass." It was to become my one and only "Mexican" dance-drama, and one of the major dances of *DAYSTAR: AN AMERICAN INDIAN WOMAN DANCES.*

It was in the spring of 1982 that I performed at the University of Colorado as a solo dance artist, at the invitation of the University's Indian Student Association, dancing "La Malinche" and my other works, the Blackfeet "Tales of Old Man," and "Spirit Woman." It was at that concert that I met Tony Shearer, who came backstage to express his regards following the concert. It was to be the beginning of a unique and amazing journey for us both—into the realms of creativity and collaboration as partners of *DAYSTAR: THE THEATRE OF ORAL TRADITIONS*—a partnership which continues today as finances and our own individual schedules permit.

In the interim between our first meeting face to face, and our future collaboration, Mr. Shearer gifted me with a copy of *The Praying Flute* both in its written text, and in the audio version performed by Tony as the storyteller. This book was to literally hypnotize my thoughts and imaginings. That summer took me to Heart Butte, Montana, to work with children. I continued to play the tape, and to read the book. On long motor journeys around the country, through Montana, the Dakotas, into Wisconsin and back, I continued to listen and experience the magic of Little Girl, Old Flute Lady, Quanab, and Altim Elut . . . a story of Indian America from an Indian heart . . . for children.

4

The teaching value of *The Praying Flute* goes without saying—it is a true Indian classic of children's literature in America—literally a masterpiece. For me personally, it is the best of the writing of Tony Shearer. It deserves to be read by all ages, in America and everywhere, but more than that, it deserves to be brought, in all its charm, to the screen, and to the live stage. Mr. Shearer's *Lord of the Dawn* became an inspiration for Louis Valdez and the El Teatro Campecino in the early 1970's, illuminating as it did the richness of the Mexican Indian heritage.

Preparations are now being made to adapt *The Praying Flute* as a stage play, to be performed by children of all ages, both Indian and non-Indian. The work of DAYSTAR is especially suited for this possibility, focusing as it does on the interweaving of interpretive movement, pantomime, and excellent staging effects. With the support of those interested in fostering the beauty and integrity of Indian America for all of us, the story would also make an intriguing first-class animated film.

The Praying Flute is now in its new and most beautiful edition. It forms the second of a trilogy of books created by Tony Shearer, which, when complete with *The Boy and The Tree,* will represent one of the most outstanding writing accomplishments by an Indian author in America.

I am honored to be associated with this book, and with Tony Shearer. *Long Live Indian America!*

Rosalie M. Jones, "Daystar"
Great Falls, Montana
February 14, 1987

ACKNOWLEDGEMENTS

I would like to offer a special thanks to Craig Stevenson and Sha Jason for allowing me space and time to complete this new edition of *The Praying Flute, Song of the Earth Mother.* And to my sister Ruth Steeves, for her special concern and her son John Moreno for his patience and support. To June Strunk for being my model, and Ken Slagle for his help down through the years. To Steve Lucero for his artistic advice, and Susan Salazar for being such a friend of "Little Girl."

Here, too, I must mention Jake White Crow and Ken and Penny Light for help in spreading the story and the song. And Eddy Box and all the Southern Utes who know and love the story, and the Lakotas who recognize "Little Girl." Thanks to the Sun Dancers who dance "Her" spirit. And perhaps more directly a thanks to the League of the Iroquois who since the days of Deganawehda have actually lived the real story of the Song of the Earth Mother . . .

Thanks to all of you.

Tony Shearer

TO THE READER

As a child, I was taught by a very wise man. I learned that the Earth is our Mother and that the Sky is our Father. This very wise teacher taught me that being Indian means that I am responsible for the spiritual welfare of the Earth Mother. He also taught me I must guard the image of womanhood and of manhood. He explained that would man and woman ever approach each other in less than a sacred manner, the Earth Herself would reflect that approach, and that She would become as corrupt and evil as the path we had chosen for each other.

Needless to say, my wise old teacher was correct. I have recently realized he was seldom, if ever, wrong.

Here then, in this little book, is the first installment of what I pray will flower into a great Earth Mother movement. I am convinced that the only way we can return to a Sacred Path is through the hearts of our children. And I pray to God it is not too late.

I have taken special care in designing each and every page. Since the book has been printed on special paper, you may find it enjoyable to paint each page. By doing so, you will be exploring the art where I have hidden little humors and some strange mysteries, and a magic formula or two.

If you enjoy the book, and I truly hope that you do, let us hear from you; drop us a card with your name and address on it and we will send you information on other Earth Mother projects.

We have also prepared a cassette taping of *Praying Flute.* It is one hour long, including the voice of a very, very ancient flute. I'm sure you will enjoy it. It is available upon your request. (More about that later.)

Now settle back and meditate, drive the shadows of fear and doubt from your mind. Pretend you are sitting beside a clear sweet brook, birds are singing, water is rattling over the stones, a pine squirrel is chattering from a branch on an ancient tree. Now . . . turn the page and begin the story.

GRANDFATHER

Old Quanab was an Indian. He was the oldest man I have ever known. No one knew for sure how old he really was, but judging from his stories, he had been alive while wild buffaloes were still on the great plains.

His home was a tepee planted in a small grove of aspens on the western slope of Bald Mountain. (He called it Spirit Mountain.) A tiny spring seeped from the ground just below his camp. We came to know that spring as Charm Springs. (He called it Pockwatchie Spring.) It was the only drinking water around these parts, cold and clear as crystal.

Outdoor people used to love to hike over the Bald Mountain trail. They would spend a whole morning getting to old Quanab's camp. They'd bring him steak, and strawberries, bake him a pie, or bring over a few fried chickens and some potato salad. Their hopes were to swap him some grub for one of his Spirit Mountain Stories.

If they were lucky, if the old man wasn't down gathering herbs on Clear Creek or fishing in Beaver Brook, they might be able to get him to tell them a story.

I could always tell when he was going to spin one of his tales. He'd load up his pipe, pour a cup of pitch-black coffee, and mosey over to his Memory Tree; an old dead aspen he used to hang his shield and flute on. He hung medicine pouches and tobacco pouches there too. He'd sit down by the tree and light his pipe and wait for all of us to make ourselves comfortable. Then he'd begin, always in the same way:

"This is a story about a place . . ."

People would sit for hours and listen to Old Quanab tell his stories. They loved that old man. They loved what he stood for, too. He was peaceful but strong, he was hard working, but loved his rest in the haunts of nature, he was happy to hear about another man's spiritual knowledge as long as that other man didn't try to impose his beliefs on Quanab, he was honest and kind, swift to help the needy and not too proud to accept a favor or a gift.

All of the "other people" called him Quanab. "We" called him Grandfather, and "we" called him Grandfather with pride. I guess I loved that old man for more reasons than I can ever tell, though the reasons that seem to be clearest now are his Spirit Mountain Stories. Those are the best memories I have of Grandfather and his Memory Tree.

Grandfather told me that long ago, before the White people came to this land, even before the Indian people were created, this land was inhabited by Little People: Pockwatchies and Tlaloques. He said those little people lived everywhere in the country, and they lived in total peace with one another. These Little People were only two inches tall, though they were very powerful little fellows. They lived in the tree tops in olden days, where they could study the stars and count the cycles of the moon.

He said the Little People were living good lives, getting along fine with one another. Then, one day, some big people showed up. These big people were not as large as you and me, they were two feet tall and were called Chanikies. The Chanikies and the Little People got along fine together. They celebrated the same days of feast and days of fast together, even attended the Sweat Lodge together. Inter-marriage was out of the question, but they could help each other enjoy life and they liked doing things together.

When the giants showed up, things became hard for the Little People and the Chanikies. The giants were the Indian people of today. Not many Indian people remember the terrible battles they waged on the Chanikies, nor the difficulty the Little People had making friends with the giants.

One day, Grandfather loaded his pipe and filled his coffee cup. I knew what was going to happen, so I hurried over to the Memory Tree. I sat down by an old stump and waited. In a moment he came over and sat down. He looked off toward the west, over the Rockies. The sun had just gone down.

"This is going to be a nighttime story," he said. Then he began . . .

LITTLE GIRL

This is a story
about a place back East.

Back beyond the
Sacramento River,
the Colorado River,
the Rio Grande,

beyond the wide Missouri, even beyond
the Mississippi and the Ohio.
Past the Monongahela
and the Allegheny River
to a place called Tawasentha,
    "Green and Silent Valley."

In Tawasentha there was an Indian Village.

In that Indian village lived a
lot of people.

One of those people was called
    "Little Girl."
It doesn't matter much what her name was,
we'll just call her "Little Girl" for now.

Little Girl liked to go out
in the woods, all by herself, alone.
Her mother would always tell her,
    "You can go out in the woods,
    but stay on your path,
    don't go too far. The woods
    are dark and deep around here,
    and it's very easy to get lost."

Little Girl learned her path.
She came to know it very well;
How it crossed the meadow,
how it passed the berry bushes and
went into the deep, dark woods.
How the old trees bent over the path.
How the light from the sun
would play through the dark shadows.
She learned the flowers, and the voices
of the birds,
the rattle of the squirrel.

But most of all, she learned that her
path ended at a big ancient tree.

Little Girl never went
beyond that tree.

She would go just that far.
There she would sit,
watch the birds and relax a little.
That old tree made her feel happy,
made her feel comfortable.

One day Little Girl went out to
her old tree friend.
She was sitting there on an old log
in the shade of the big tree, watching
a butterfly, listening to a bird sing.

Suddenly, something appeared over
in the grass.
It was only a flash and then it was gone.
    "What was that?" she thought.
Then all at once something appeared
on the log,
just WOOP, and it was there.
She looked . . . it was a little man,
about two inches tall, with a
wrinkled old face.
She was a-looking at him and he was
a-looking at her.
    "Who are . . ."
Before she could even finish her
question he was gone like a puff.
She looked around, over here
and over there.
She couldn't see him any place.
Just then she heard a tiny voice:
    "Look here," it said.

She looked up, and there he was,
sitting on a branch right above her head.
It was the same little old man, about
two inches tall.
His face was all wrinkled,
he wore buckskin clothes
and tiny, tiny bird feathers
were in his hair.
The look on his face didn't look as
if he was smiling, but he didn't
look as if he was frowning either.
He sat and looked at her.
Then Little Girl said,
    "Who are you?"
Thoom, he appeared right on the
tip of her big toe.
    "Well," she said,
    "Who are you now?"
He looked at her with a very serious
expression on his face and he said
    "Little Girl, I'm in a big hurry.

I've come to tell you something you're
supposed to know. Now, I don't have
much time. I've got to hurry.
I've been sent to 'open your eyes.' You're
the one that has been chosen for this.
We've got to hurry, though,
you see. Let me get up on your
shoulder. There, that's better, now we can go."
The little man was on her shoulder and
Little Girl's eyes were
as big as silver dollars.
She said, "Well, what are we going
to do; where are we going to go?"
"Well now," he said,

"You just follow my directions and every
thing will be good. You see
over there?"

"Yes."

"That's a rose bush, that's a primrose bush. You walk on over there."

"All right."

She got up and walked over to the rose bush.

"Now," he said, "look on over that way. You see over there? You see that big old rock?"

"Yes," she said, "I see it."

"Well, get walking. Don't just stand there. We've got to hurry. I haven't got much time. I'm in a big hurry, can't stay here very long, you know, and talk to you. I've got things to do, lots of things, so hurry on up."

Little Girl walked over to the big rock as fast as she could. When she got there the little man said,

"Now, walk around and you'll
see something . . . see there? There's
the creek bed. We've got to cross
that creek. Be careful
or you'll step in the water."
Sure enough, she stepped right
into the water.
    "Now don't do that any more!
You got your feet wet, and we're
going to a place where
you're not going to be able
to dry out.
Be careful and climb up
this hill," he said.
She climbed as fast as she could up the little hill.
When she got to the top she looked
down on the other side: there, in the gray
rocks was a dark hole:

A cave, very dark and very wet,
with moss and ferns
growing all around it.
Slowly she climbed down to the
mouth of the cave and looked inside
the dark hole.

"Are we going in there?" she asked.
"Yes, Little Girl," he said, "we're
going down in that dark hole.
You've got to start shutting
off your head, and start
learning how to think with
your heart. We are
going very deep into that hole,
and there's no light down there.
If you try to walk with
your head you'll never make
it all the way. You've got to
walk with your heart."
"What's down there?" she asked.
"Now you listen," he said, "you listen
just a minute before we take another
step. My name is Quill and I'm
a Pockwatchie. Don't tell me you
never heard of Pockwatchies before
'cause I know you never
heard of Pockwatchies before
'cause you're the first one to

be told about Pockwatchies.
But before you come up
out of that dark hole
you're going to know a lot
about Pockwatchies and
Tlaloques. You're going to
know about Earth Spirits,
and, Little Girl, you're going
to be able to walk with
your heart. Do you understand?"

"Yes,"
said Little Girl with a little voice,

"I think I understand. I hope I do."
"All right," said Quill,
start walking, and remember,
don't try to walk with
your head. Walk with your heart
and you'll get through this
darkness a lot easier."

They started down into the dark hole.
As they walked along it got darker and darker.
The cave smelled of newborn, it was
damp and warm and very good.
As Little Girl walked further she
learned to walk with her heart, and it
wasn't scary at all.
Once in a while she would hear a little voice
saying something to comfort her,

    "You're doing real good, Little Girl."

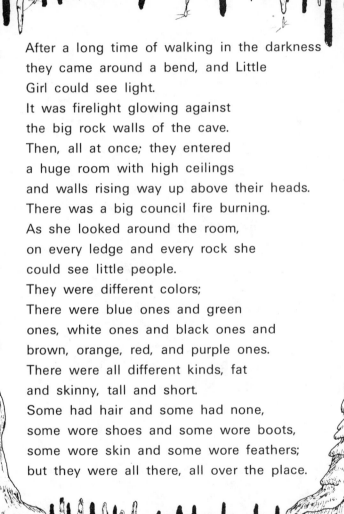

After a long time of walking in the darkness
they came around a bend, and Little
Girl could see light.
It was firelight glowing against
the big rock walls of the cave.
Then, all at once; they entered
a huge room with high ceilings
and walls rising way up above their heads.
There was a big council fire burning.
As she looked around the room,
on every ledge and every rock she
could see little people.
They were different colors;
There were blue ones and green
ones, white ones and black ones and
brown, orange, red, and purple ones.
There were all different kinds, fat
and skinny, tall and short.
Some had hair and some had none,
some wore shoes and some wore boots,
some wore skin and some wore feathers;
but they were all there, all over the place.

As Little Girl looked at all of them
she became frightened.
She said,
    "Quill, Quill!"
Quill said,
    "Don't be scared now,
    remember, think with your heart."
    "There must be thousands of
    them," she said.
    "Oh yes," said Quill, "there are more
    than that. They're playing their
    games and they're doing their
    ceremonies and their dances, and all of that."
Little Girl could hear their little drums
beating their little songs.
She could see them doing their little
dances around their little fires.
Some of them were sitting back, talking
little talk with each other.
They were laughing at their little jokes

playing little games.
You can't imagine how many little games
Pockwatchies and Tlaloques can play.
Little Girl relaxed and she said,
    "Quill, what are they?"
He said,
    "Well, like I told you, these are
    Pockwatchies and Tlaloques. Now
    listen carefully, 'cause I'm in a
    hurry. I'll tell you one time
    and you've got to remember.
    I'm going to tell you fast, so listen.
    See those green ones?"
                    "YES."
    "Those green ones, those are
    Pockwatchies. They are the
    guardians of the grass; and
    the big green ones; they are
    tree guardians. You see
    the blue ones over there?"
                    "YES."

35

"Those are Tlaloques, water guardians.
The blue ones are the guardians
of springs, and little creeks,
not big rivers. You see the
purple ones? They're the
guardians of the big wide rivers.
See the brown ones?"

"YES."

"Well, those are more Pockwatchies.
That's one of my cousins over there.
You see, the one with the
big nose, that's my cousin.
He's got a story all of his own.
The brown ones are guardians
of the soil, they make
corn and beans, squash and
mushrooms grow.
The white Pockwatchies are guardians
of the Mountains. They
are ancient spirits, old and

wise. They were before the
beginning and they will be
after the end. You find
them up in the mountains,
living in the cliffs. Some
people call them
                    'Echo.'
So, you see, there are guardians
for everything on the Earth. And
these are the guardians;
Pockwatchies and Tlaloques.
Do you understand, Little Girl?"

"Well, I sort of understand, Quill"
she said.
"That's the way it's supposed to be,"
said Quill.

At that moment everything became
very silent, very still.
Little Girl looked to see what had happened.
All of the Pockwatchies and Tlaloques
were standing very still.
They were all looking at a crack in
the wall of the cave.
A bright light was streaming out of
the crack.
Little Girl almost stopped breathing.
Then she said,
    "Quill!"
    "Sh," said Quill,
    "don't say a word, the chief's coming!"
From the crack in the wall came another little man.
He looked very noble and wise.
He glowed with a strange magic light.
His skin looked very much like hers.
It was kind of . . . kind of red.
His hair was very black and
it was braided.

He wore a great feathered headdress
and his buckskin was snow
white with BLACK and RED beads sewn on it.
As he walked toward her she went down
on her knees so she would be closer to him.
Then she heard her heart tell her to put
out her hand.

She did as her heart said, and he
stepped up on her hand, and
she stood up.

There she stood in the cave, holding
the little Pockwatchie in her hand.

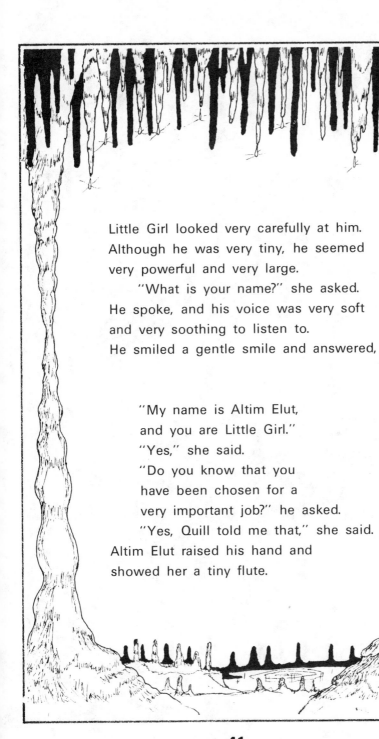

Little Girl looked very carefully at him.
Although he was very tiny, he seemed
very powerful and very large.

"What is your name?" she asked.
He spoke, and his voice was very soft
and very soothing to listen to.
He smiled a gentle smile and answered,

"My name is Altim Elut,
and you are Little Girl."
"Yes," she said.
"Do you know that you
have been chosen for a
very important job?" he asked.
"Yes, Quill told me that," she said.
Altim Elut raised his hand and
showed her a tiny flute.

"This is a flute, Little Girl.
When you leave this cave
you will find a white
flute laying on the ground.
It is yours forever."
"Thank you very much," said Little Girl.
"You are welcome, and we
are happy that you are
the one who was chosen," he said.

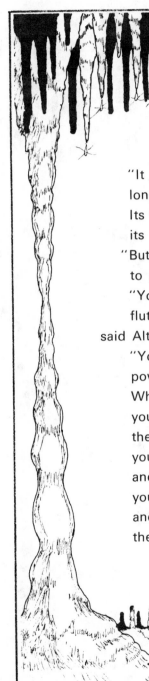

"It took us a very
long time to make your flute.
Its voice is very wonderful,
its spirit very pure."
"But I don't know how
to play a flute," said Little Girl.
"Your flute is not a playing
flute, yours is a 'Praying Flute,'"
said Altim Elut.
"You must understand its
power and its purpose.
When you Pray with
your flute you're calling
the Earth Mother's guardians,
you are calling the Pockwatchies
and Tlaloques. In other words,
you are talking to the trees
and rivers, the flowers and
the seeds of the 'unborn.'"

"That is very beautiful," said
Little Girl, "but I don't know
any tunes."
"Listen," said Altim Elut, "listen."
With that he lifted his flute to his
mouth and blew.
The music rose like magic and filled
the dark cave with a delightful song.
The sound was so sweet it brought
tears to Little Girls' eyes.
When Altim Elut had finished his song
he smiled and said,
"That is the
'Song of the Earth Mother.'
It is the oldest song in all the world."
"It was so beautiful,"
said Little Girl, "I
hope I can remember it."
"You will remember it,"
smiled Altim Elut,

44

"In a moon or two
you will be Praying
it like an old master."
Then Altim Elut told Little Girl about
the spirits of the flowers and the butterflies.
He told her about cactus and lilies, and how
they long to be loved by people, told her how
the Earth Mother is the true
Mother to all things that live.
Altim Elut told Little Girl about the
creation of all things, and how in the beginning,
long before man was created,
the Great Spirit had created
the Little People and appointed them
the Guardians of the Earth Mother.
"Flowers and Trees," said he,
"do not speak, but they
have hearts and spirits
just like you and
just like me. They

can feel your love,
hear your heart's
message. And 'we,'
the guardians,
were created to
remind all things
of their relationship;
and to never, never
forget Earth Mother.
She is a living thing,
very, very important in
the Great Creation of
the Great Spirit.
Do you understand,
Little Girl?"
"Well," said Little Girl,
"I sort of understand.
Yes, I understand
with my heart. You
protect the earth, the
Earth Mother and all things
that live on her."
"That's good enough

for now," said Altim Elut.
"Come over here, over
to this big stone wall.
Just walk to that crack
you see there.
    Now look in the crack," said Altim Elut.
Little Girl leaned down and looked in the
crack in the cave wall.
Inside the crack was a beautiful world.
She saw all sorts of beautiful things.
She saw her valley Tawasentha, her
people; all happy,
all living in harmony.
She drew back, and with a big
smile she said,
    "That's beautiful.
    How does it happen?"
    "Don't worry about how it
    happens," he said, "There
    are many things you
    will never understand,
    but they happen anyway.

Did you like what you saw?"
"Oh yes, I saw all the
good things."
"Very good," said Altim Elut.
"Now come over here.
Do you see that other crack?"

"Yes," she said.
"I want you to look
in that crack," said Altim Elut.
Little Girl quickly leaned down to look in
the crack. But when she looked she jumped back
with a shock.
"That's terrible," she said.
"Yes, yes, that is very
terrible. I am sorry
you had to see it.
That is what the world
would look like if
there was no spirit."
"I don't ever want to see
that again," she said.

"No, no one would want
to look at *that,* especially
if they could see it as things
were meant to be," he said.
Then Altim Elut asked Little Girl to put
him down by the crack in the wall
from where he had come.
He said,
"You have seen both cracks
in the wall. You know the
difference. You are
the only one who knows.
Pray the Flute when
you find someone who
doesn't know about
us, and we will come
and teach them.
Now I leave you.
Your Flute is very important.
Your job will be very
difficult. Remember to think
with your heart.

Good luck and goodbye."
Altim Elut smiled and turned, and
walked away into the little crack in the
big stone wall.
His glowing light slowly faded.
Not a sound came from one Pockwatchie.
Not a sound came from one Tlaloque.
They stood very still and smiled very
gently at Little Girl.
Then Quill appeared beside her.
    "It's time to get going!" he said.
Little Girl waved goodbye to all
the little people,
and all the little people waved goodbye to her.
She put Quill on her shoulder and
the two of them traveled upward through
the long darkness, 'till they saw the
bright light of the happy sun.

Then Quill told Little Girl,
    "I've been in a hurry
    since I met you.
    That's because I'm
    always in a hurry.
    Now, what I want you
    to do is to remember
    everything you can about what
    has happened today.
    Every word is important.
    Will you do that?"
    "I'll do that," said Little Girl.
    "Good," said Quill, "Now,
    look over there,"
She looked, and there on the ground,
lying just outside the cave, was a
pure White Flute.
    "Oh, that's my Flute," she said.
When she looked back,

                    Quill was gone.

FLUTE LADY

Little Girl took her Flute and
started back to her village.
She went back past the creek;
she didn't step
in the water this time.
She went back past the big rock and
the primrose bush, back past
her tree friend.
She stopped there for a minute; that
ancient tree looked even older now.

Then she went down her path,
through the dark woods, past the berry
bushes, over the meadows, and home.
When she was there she said,
    "Mother, today . . ."
She told her mother the whole story.
Her mother laughed and said,
    "Oh, that's very nice, Little Girl.
    It's wonderful to have
    such a good imagination.
    But there aren't really any
    Little People, are there?"
Then her mother heard the sweet voice
of the Flute and she started
to change her mind . . . a little bit.

Little Girl found a small hill
that overlooked the valley of Tawasentha.
Every morning

and every evening,
she would stand up there on
the hill and Pray her Flute.
She would Pray it to the East.
She would Pray it to the West.
Sometimes Little Girl
would Pray it to the North and the South.
When she would Pray the Flute
she would always think of "little
ol' Quill," and of the things Altim
Elut had told her that magic
day down in the dark hole.
One day an old man came running
into camp.
He was all excited.
    "You know what I just found
    out?" he said,
    "Down by the river I saw
    a spirit, a River Spirit.
    He was just a little fellow,
    'bout two inches tall. He
    was purple."

Then the people started to say,
    "You know,
        that River's got a spirit."
Little Girl Prayed some more;
in the morning and
in the evening.

Sure enough, it wasn't long and two
women came into camp:
    "We just saw a Tree Spirit."
said one.
    "And a Grass Spirit,"
said the other woman.
    "And that Tree Spirit talked to
    me," said the first woman.
    "He talked to me first,"
said the other woman.
    "He said trees have spirits
        and the grass has a spirit . . ."

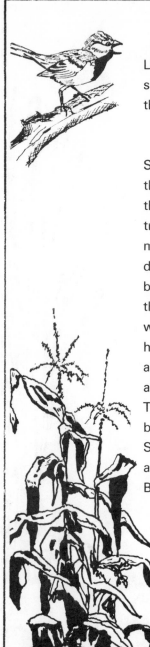

Little Girl didn't say anything,
she just Prayed her Flute and
thought to herself,
    "Oh, they are doing it,
    they are *really* doing it."
Soon all of the people learned
that the Earth has a spirit and
that all things, like
trees, grass, rivers, flowers,
mountains (echo), lakes, springs
deer, frogs, gophers, squirrels,
bears, dogs, cats, and all
the other things in the whole
world, in the whole universe,
have spirit
and
are related to each other.
Time went on and Little Girl grew up and
became a woman.
She went and got married
and had children of her own.
But she kept on Praying her Flute anyway.

Every morning she was out there on her
little hill overlooking the valley of Tawasentha.
Every evening she was out
Praying some more with her Pockwatchie Flute.
The Flute had a wonderful voice,
and a pure spirit was inside its music.

They didn't call her Little Girl anymore.
They now called her Flute Lady.
Flute Lady became known to everyone;
every tribe of Indian People knew about
Flute Lady.
When they would see her at dawn,
headed up the little hill, it made
them feel good because they knew
in a little while they would be
hearing the "Song of the Earth Mother"
They had all come to know
what that meant.

OLD FLUTE LADY

"What color are Mountain Spirits?"
asked one man.

"White," said the other man.

"How big are Mountain Spirits?"
asked that man.

"About two inches tall, maybe a little
bigger," said the other man.

"Well," said that man, "a
whole load of giant Mountain
Spirits has just landed over at
Plymouth Rock."

"Giant Mountain Spirits?"
"Yes, giant Mountain Spirits."
"How giant?"
"Big as you, maybe bigger."
"Where did they come from?"
"Up out of the sea, they just
came out of the waters,
from the ocean."
"There's something fishy about
this," said one of the chiefs,
"We'd better go on over and
find out what this is all about.
I never heard of giant Mountain
Spirits coming up out of the
the ocean."
So a bunch of Indians went
over to Plymouth Rock to find out
about what was happening.
They were gone for quite a while.
Then the word came back to
Tawasentha . . .
                    "WHITE MEN"
White men were coming from the east
in big ships with big sails.
They were landing on the ocean shore.
They were building houses.
That's the story the people at Tawasentha heard.
At first they didn't know

what to make of all this.
But the stories kept coming and
the people kept listening.
They heard these White People had
beards; well, the men had beards.
They heard these White People had
all sorts of things the Indians had never heard of.
They had axes and saws, nails
and hammers, guns and glass;
they even had some glass beads.

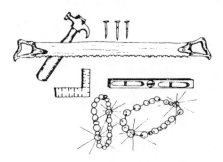

Those glass beads were interesting
to the people of Tawasentha.
So, along about autumn, they got
together a bunch of turkeys
and corn and squash and beans,
pumpkins and cranberries,
and they said,

"Let's all of us go over
to Plymouth Rock and
celebrate 'Earth Mother Day'
with those White People."
"That's a good idea,"
said a woman, "I want
to see those men with
hair on their faces."
"I agree," said another
woman, "maybe we can
swap some corn for some
of those glass beads."
The chief thought he might
get himself an axe or
a hammer and some nails.

63

That's how it happened.
All the Indian People went over
to meet the White People at
Plymouth Rock.
When the White People saw all the
Indians coming, they went out to meet them.
The first White Man said,
     "It's good to see you folks.
     We thought you would
     never come over."
     "Well," said the Chief, "we've
     been busy all summer
     growing our crops and
     hunting deer and all that."

The White Man said,
        "Come on in and sit down,
        you're all welcome. Would
        you like to see my . . . glass beads?"
The Chief said,
        "We came over to celebrate
        Earth Mother Day with
        you. We brought along a
        bunch of turkeys and
        corn and squash and
        other things. We thought you folks
        might like to share our
        gifts with us. What
        color are your . . . glass beads?"
        "What's Earth Mother Day?" asked
        the White Man.
So one of the Indian Women told
them about the Spirit of the Earth
Mother, told them about the Spirit of
the land, how the 'Great Spirit'
rewards people for their
labors in the field with the
gift of the harvest.
One of the White Women said,
        "That's giving 'Thanks.' "
Someone else said,
        "We should call this day
        'Thanksgiving Day'."

That's how *that* happened.
The chief came back with a
hammer and some nails.
His wife came back with a
whole sack of pretty glass beads.
That was the story Flute Lady heard.
Then she heard there were Indians going
over to Plymouth Rock and they were building houses.
More people were coming
from across the sea and they
were building houses too.

They built, oh, about ten houses at first.
Then they built twelve or thirteen houses.
Finally they stopped building houses
and they built one big building.
Then they built other big buildings.
Then they tore down some of the houses
and they built more buildings.
Still more buildings were built.
Flute Lady heard about all of this.
She heard about the buildings being built.
The buildings went all over,
they were being built by
Red People,
Black People,
White People,
and Brown People.
Then there were Yellow People coming
and they were building them too.
Some of the people were digging into the
earth and taking out minerals,
and oil and all sorts of things.
Then they started building factories;
the factories were built up alongside the rivers.
Then they built bridges across the rivers,
and houses went everywhere,
just everywhere you can imagine.
There were more and more houses.
Flute Lady was growing older and older.

The houses were getting bigger and bigger.
There were more factories and more big buildings.
One day Flute Lady went up and looked
over to the east—there were nothing but houses
everywhere,
and big buildings.
The hills were just covered with houses
for people to live in;
and factories for people to work in.
There were bridges across the rivers.
Then there were fences;
fences to keep things in
and fences to keep things out.
There were buildings inside the fences
and buildings outside the fences.
Fences were running everywhere.
Roads and highways
were all over the place.
Flute Lady would climb to the top of Indian Hill.
There she would raise her Flute and Pray.
But there was so much rumble, so
much vibration, she could hardly
hear the sweet voice.

"Don't be playing your
flute so early in the morning. A man's got
to get his sleep,
you know," said one fellow.

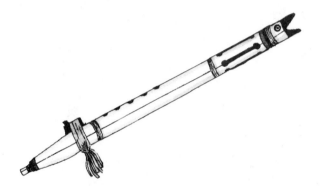

"Don't be playing your
flute in the evenings,
it bothers my television
show," said another.
"Why don't you take your
flute out in the country?
Play it out there where
it doesn't bother people."

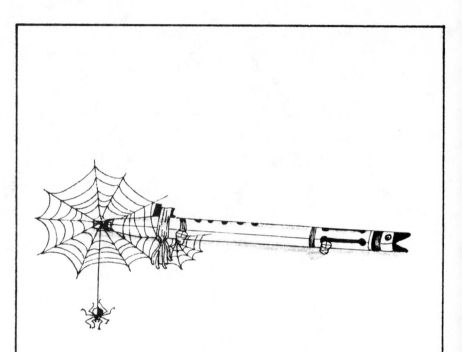

The Flute started to hang on
the wall, sometimes for days,
sometimes for weeks.
One day Flute Lady went to Pray,
and a strange thing had happened.
A little Black and Red spider
had built a web over the mouth
of the Flute, and had made
a nest inside the other end.

Flute Lady was now Old Flute Lady,
and she didn't want to disturb that
little spider.
So she just said,
        "I guess that spider
        has more use for
        the Flute than anyone else."
Besides, she hadn't seen a spider
in a long time.
At night she could see the lights
of the city glowing bright.
She could hear the motors of the automobiles
coming down the road,
and trucks going this way and that way.
All of these things were there and
sometimes it was hard to see the sunrise
because there was an awful lot of smoke in the air.
No one seemed to know and no one seemed
to care anymore.
No one seemed to know that all things in the
universe are related and all things in the
universe have a spirit.
It was on Earth Mother Day, Thanksgiving,
that someone heard the rumor,
        "I heard that Old Flute Lady
        died. Did you hear about
        that?" asked someone.
        "No, I didn't hear about that.

But she was getting
very old. I haven't
heard her flute for a
long, long time. Maybe
she went and died,"
said another.

"She was a good old
woman, but she had too
many old ideas. She was
always talking about
Pockwatchies and those
'Other' things."

AND
So it was said,
Old Flute Lady is dead . . .

OLD, OLD FLUTE LADY

The trees were cut down,
Where once a dark woods had stood,
now there were cities.
Where fields had once been,
now there were factories.
Along the rivers
there were factories.
In the towns there were factories.

Some children couldn't even see the stars.
Then people all over the land
started to say things like,

"Cough, cough. You know, we
can't breathe very good any
more in the cities."
                           and
"You know, we're having touble
getting water to drink."
It got worse and worse, and
it got even worse, if you can imagine that.
The people everywhere were wondering what
was happening to the earth.
Some people were saying,

"What we've got to do is to do something
about the land, let's have a meeting.
We've got to do something
about the water, let's have another meeting.
We've got to do something
about the air."

Well, they got together and they went up
and they looked at the land and they said
to a farmer,
"Why isn't there corn growing
in that field?"
The farmer said,
"The reason there isn't corn
growing in that field is the
water isn't any good to put on
the corn, so there are just weeds
growing out there, and they're not
growing very good."
Then another man said,
"Well, why isn't there wheat growing over there?"
The farmer said,
"The reason there's no wheat growing
over there is because the dirt is polluted."
The people said,
"Well, that's the way it is all over the land."
Dr. Toningworm was a scientist, and
one day he came down to the River.
He put on a pair of sanitary rubber
gloves, and sanitary rubber boots.
He waded out in that River.

He opened a sanitary bottle and took
some water from the River.
Then he went back to his sanitary
laboratory at the university, opened
    the sanitary bottle, put one
    drop of water on the sanitary glass slide,
    and placed the glass slide into the
    electronic microscope.

He looked inside the viewer, studied it for
a couple of minutes.
Then he looked up at the student
that stood across the table from him.
Dr. Toningworm said,
    "That River is dead."
The student said,
    "That River is dead?"
The student went out and told someone,
    "That River is dead."
That person went and told someone else,
    "That River is dead."
Pretty soon the newspaper got ahold of the
story and they put out a banner headline,

"THAT RIVER
IS DEAD"

People stood back and they looked
at that dead River and they said,
        "Well, what happened to the River?"
Then big signs were put up that said,
        "Keep away from this dead River, it's bad for you."
The water wasn't fit to even touch.
There was nothing alive.
The spirit was gone.
Then they looked and trees, big
trees that stood along the River, started to fall over.

They just came crashing to the ground
at night with great sounds
and frightened people.
The trees were falling down and people were
standing there looking and they said,
        "What happened to those trees?"
        "Well, the trees can't stand the
        bad water either. They drink the
        water and they just fall over."
There was no grass growing along
the River either.
Nothing grew near the River; the
people stood back.
They started to move their houses away.
There were things piled, like trash,
alongside the rivers and alongside
the highways and near the bridges.

All the fences had pieces of paper
and things hooked to them and it was
terrible looking and trash cans were turned
over in the alleys and the water
would drain down into the dead River.
Even the springs in the high mountains
were dying.
Up in the mountains the air was so
thick and so polluted that
the trees couldn't breathe.

"You know, there's an old woman,
an old Indian woman that lives out there,
somewhere; over by that funny hill.
Old Indian Hill they call it.
She's got a flute. They say
that if she plays the flute, she
can bring the rivers back alive, and the trees."
"That's an old Indian story,"
said a man, "It's not true."
"It's true," said someone,
"but she's dead, I heard
she went and died."
"Maybe she didn't die,"
said another.
"She's got an old, old
flute. Sweet voice, I heard."
said a man.

"That flute," said
a student, "might be the
magic we need to save the world."
"Well, we don't believe that,"
said someone.
Dr. Toningworm said, "Well,
we'd better believe it.
Find that old woman!"
So they went looking for
Old Flute Lady . . .
The went from house to house
and they said,
    "Hey, are you an Indian?"
and the person said,
        "Well, yeah, I'm an Indian."
        "Well, have you got a flute?"
        "No, I don't have a flute, I've got a drum.
        I know about an old woman; she
        lives over at Indian Hill, she's got a flute."
        Dr. Toningworm said, "Come on with us.
        We'll find that old woman, look for her!"
So they went through every house
along the rivers and up in
the hills looking for Old, Old Flute Lady.
Finally they came to an old house, they knocked
on the door and an old, old Indian man
came out. He was all in braids and he
had feathers in his headdress, you know,
just like the old times.

Dr. Toningworm said,
    "Old man, do you have a flute?
    Do you know that old woman that
    has a flute and plays it?"
The old Indian said,
    "I don't want to speak to you."
    They said, "Well, old man,
    why is that? Don't you see we've
    got to find that old woman?"

He said, "I don't want to speak to you."
They said, "Well, old man . . ."
The old man became angry. He said,

"Go away from my door, go away.
Go away from my door, I don't want
to speak to you!"
"Well, what's that old man angry about?"
the student asked.
Dr. Toningworm said, "Well, you know,
he could be angry
because we killed his river."

On they went, and pretty soon they
saw that funny hill that sat where the
meadow used to be, you know, where the
primrose bush was once, where the old
rock had been, and where Quill once found
Little Girl.
Well, they went up there, and there was
                    INDIAN HILL.
At the foot of the hill was a
little old house made the old way.
They knocked on the door, and for a while
there was no sound.
Then the door opened.
There was Little Girl.
She was now
"Old, Old Indian Woman."

Her face was very wrinkled and her
hair was very gray.
Her hands were all wrinkled too.
But she had that look in her eyes as if
she would forever be Little Girl.
Dr. Toningworm said,

"Are you the Old Indian Woman that has the flute?"
She said, "Why, yes. You
didn't come to take my Flute?"
He said, "No . . . no . . . we're through taking things.

We're going to ask you a favor, Old
Indian Woman. We hear that your flute,
if you play it, can bring the
spirit back to the river, and the
spirit back to the trees, back to the land."
"I didn't think anyone wanted
to heart that Flute ever
again," said Old Flute Lady.
"Will you play it?" asked Dr. Toningworm.
"It's not a playing flute,"
she said, "It's a Praying Flute.
Altim Elut gave this Flute
to me a long, long time ago.
He told me it would always work.
But, you see, now-a-days
people can't hear the old
voices, the echos from the past.
People now-a-days are very busy,
and besides, it's hard
to hear anything but noise."
"Will you Pray it for us?"
asked Dr. Toningworm.
"Well, I don't know,"
she said.
"Old Flute Lady, please come, hurry,
said Dr. Toningworm, "We need
you badly."
They hurried the old woman outside.
They took her up on the hill.
They helped her up the hill and she
had the Flute in her hand.

When she got there they said,
    "Pray, Pray the Flute."
    "All right," she said.
She lifted the Flute up through the smoke-
filled air, and she looked over the polluted earth.
She said,
    "All right, this is the song
    that comes from your Earth Mother.
    This is the oldest song in all the world."
As she Prayed, they listened to the song
and all of them thought,
    "That is a beautiful song,
    but it sounds so . . . so . . . sad now."
The Old Indian Woman Prayed the song and
then she stopped; she waited and she waited.
Dr. Toningworm said,
    "Play it again.
    Maybe they didn't hear you."
    "All right, I'll play it again," she said.
She played it again.
She prayed the whole song,
and nothing happened.
    "Let me do it once more," she said.
She climbed up to the very top of the hill.
She pointed it toward the east
where the sun rises.
She Prayed it again.
She pointed it toward the west
where the sun sets.
She Prayed it again.

Nothing happened.
　　"Well," said Dr. Toningworm, "What
　　we've got to do is get this woman
　　to the television station,
　　put her on world-wide television and
　　get that song all over the world
　　so that everyone will hear
　　it. Maybe the earth spirits will
　　hear it too, and come
　　back to help us."
　　"Oh, yes, they'll hear it."
　　said Old, Old Flute Lady, "I'm
　　sure they will."

　　　　　　　　　　　So she lifted her
　　　　　　　　　　　Ancient Flute and
　　　　　　　　　　　Prayed it on television.
　　　　　　　　　　　It was broadcast all over the world,
　　　　　　　　　　　but nothing happened.

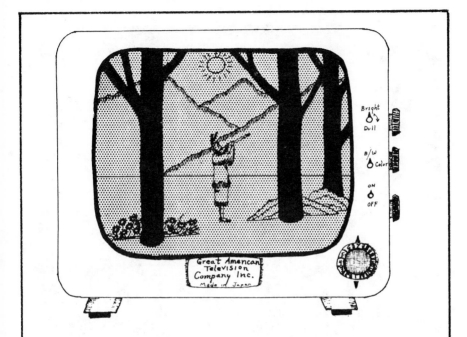

"We're missing a lot of places,"
Dr. Toningworm said,
   "I tell you what we've got to do.
   We've got to get her up in the air.
   Get her up!"
So she lifted her
Ancient Flute and
Prayed it on television.
It was broadcast all over the world,
but nothing happened.
   "We're missing a lot of places,"
Dr. Toningworm said.
   "I tell you what we've got to do.
   We've got to get her up in the air.
   Get her up!"

The large countries of the world
got together and built a great
rocket. It was shaped sort of
like a flute. They put a satellite
on it for the old woman to get into.
They gave her a microphone
and told her how to use it.
They put two giant speakers
up on the nose cone
and sent her clear up above the
earth and around the moon.

She Prayed the song up through the Universe.
From the moon she could see
the beautiful sphere—
so blue, silently
moving through space.
    "My Mother," she sighed,
    "My Mother."
She saw not one Pockwatchie,
not one Tlaloque.
    Her splashdown was in
    the Pacific, and the Navy
    Boys picked her up.
    They told her the news:

"We still haven't heard from them."
She said, "Yes, I noticed. It
looks like this ocean is dying, too."
They brought her back to San Francisco.
As she passed under the Golden Gate, she
could almost see the bridge above.
They put her on a Bulldog Bus and sent
her back to Indian Hill.
All across the land she traveled through
the towns and she met the people. The
people seemed to be confused.
They looked around and
they didn't know what to think
about what was happening.
The people talked to her.
They said,

    "Old, Old Flute Lady," (that's what they called her
    now.) "Old, Old Flute Lady, can't you make
    the spirits come back?"
    "Well, I Prayed my Flute," she said.
    "I went clear out through space.
    They sent me all the way past
    the moon to see if the earth spirits
    were out there, but they weren't there.
    The rivers are still dying, the trees are
    still falling."
The people sighed and agreed,
    "Yes, we know about all of that."

Then one little boy asked her,
     "Flute Lady, when you were out
     by the moon, could you see the stars?"
     She said, "Yes, son, I could see the stars."
A tear swelled in the little
boy's eyes as he said,
     "It's good to know the
     stars are still there.
     Do they really twinkle?"
     "YES," she said,
     "They used to twinkle
     for all people in the
     world, but that was
     a long, long time ago."
     "Do you think I will ever
     get to see the stars?"
he asked.
Old Flute Lady looked at her Flute, then at
the little boy.
She remembered Altim Elut, the Pockwatchie that glowed.
She wondered what ever had happened.
to the guardians of the Earth Mother.
She wondered where they had gone.
Then she looked into the
eyes of the child.
     "Maybe," she said,
     "Maybe it's not too late."

As she traveled eastward toward
Tawasentha she crossed over
the Great Rivers of this land;
        She Crossed:
        The Sacramento River,
        The Colorado River
        The Rio Grande
        The Plat River
        The Missouri River
        The Mississippi River
        The Ohio River
        The Monongahela River
        AND
        The Allegheny River
to old Tawasentha, and her little
house at Indian Hill.
She lit her candle,
sat down in her old chair,
and layed her Praying Flute on the table.

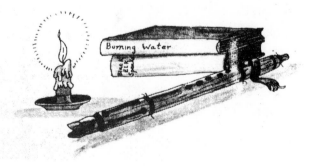

94

Leaning back in her old chair
she thought to herself,
she remembered the words
Altim Elut had said that
wonderful day down in the Cave,
     "Flowers and Trees," said he,
     "do not speak, but they
     have hearts and spirits
     just like you and
     just like me. They
     can feel your love,
     hear your heart's
     message.
     Never, never forget
     your Earth Mother.
     She is a very, very important
     part in the Great Creation
     of the Great Spirit."
     "I have failed," she said.
     "If I had prayed my flute,
     regardless of what people said,
     if I had told everyone in
     the whole wide world about
     the Little People, the Earth Spirits,
     if I had done it right
     none of this would have
     happened. I'm ashamed.
     I did it all wrong."

Then she said aloud,
"I'm old, and I'm tired, and
there is no sense in trying any longer."
She thought,
"I think I am going to die; yes
I think it's time to die."
The more she thought about it,
the better it seemed.
So, she died.
That's right, she just slumped back in her
old chair and she died.
Just as she was starting to leave her
body she heard a very angry voice say,

"GET BACK IN YOUR BODY, YOU
CAN'T DIE YET, IT'S NOT TIME!
GET BACK IN THAT OLD BODY AND STAY THERE!"

It was Quill, standing on the
table just a little ways from her flute.
"Quill," she said, "you've come back."
"Come back? Come Back?!
I never left. I've been watching
this whole thing. It's working
out just fine. You're doing
real good. But now we
have to hurry. There's not
much time left. It's time
for Earth Spirit Action, come on!"

"But Quill," she said, "I'm too
old, and Quill, I'm tired."
"Nobody's old enough yet,"
said Quill, "And you haven't even
begun to work, so don't tell me you're tired."
"But Quill," the Old Woman started.
"But nothing," said Quill, "Old Indian
Woman, get ahold of me, quick, let me
climb on your hand."
She stood up just as fast as she could.
He said, "Now, we've got to hurry,
because I'm in a BIG HURRY. Get me in your hand."
When she put her hand down he jumped on it
and said,
"Get the Flute; now come on outside.
Hurry up, I haven't got much time."
She said, "Well, I'm going just
as fast as I can, but I can't move
like I used to."
He said, "See that, down there,
down there by that bridge?"
"Yes."
"Well, get on over there across
the bridge, come on."
She was walking just as fast as she could,
but she was old.
She crossed the bridge and then Quill said,
"Now, see over there?"

"You see—that's the city dump."
"Quill, wait!" she said with a start.
"This is what I saw, years ago, down
in the cave the first day I ever met you.
This is what I saw in the
bad crack in the wall!"
"Yes, I know that, but
we've got to hurry, we haven't
got much time. Hurry, hurry on."
The old woman hurried just as
fast as she could.
She found the highest mound
in the dump and started to climb
to the very top of it.
She kicked her way up
the mound, through the waste of
broken bottles, old tin cans, refrigerators,
discarded TV sets, plastic boxes, old
battered plastic trucks and dolls.
Suddenly she noticed something
sticking up out of a heap of
trash. It was a book that someone
had thrown away.
The old woman paused and
took the book from the heap.
She wiped it off, thumbed
through it. Then she said,

"Quill, did you know about
this book?"
The little man only motioned
her up on the mound. He said,
"Keep it, put it in your
pocket, you can read it
later. Now, get going on
up there, we have to hurry."
When they reached the top Quill said,
"Well, this is where
we start."

"What are we going to do?
I've tooted my Flute everywhere.
I Prayed, all my life I Prayed
with the Flute."
Quill said, "Well, no one
said you didn't. You're
doing real fine. Everything's
working out real good.
But now, now things are
going to become hard for you.
That is why you were chosen, for this day."
"But I'm old, and I'm tired," she said.
He said, "Nobody's old enough,
and you haven't started to be
tired yet."
"What have I got to do, Quill?"
He said, "Little Girl, Old Flute Lady, you
have to Pray your Flute.
You can't do it in a satellite
and you can't do it on the television.
You've got to go to the
                    CHILDREN.
You've go to go right into the schoolroom,
you've got to take that Flute.
You can't go in and ask anybody
if you can. You just walk in.
When you walk in the room, they'll
know who you are. Do you hear me?"

"Yes, Quill, I hear you, but . . ."
"Don't worry about food, you'll
have food to eat and you'll have a place
to sleep, all the time.
So don't worry about that,"
said Quill.
"All right, Quill," she said.
"Now, here's what you do," said Quill.
"You go into the class room.
Walk in, don't say a word to anyone.
You just lift up the Flute
and Pray it, the whole song.
Then the hearts of the children will open,
and when their hearts are open
we'll jump inside."
She said, "You'll jump inside?!"
"Yep, we're gonna jump inside.
All of us, every Earth Guardian, is
standing by. There are millions of us,
maybe billions of us, just waiting for you to come there
and Pray the Flute and open the hearts,
so we can jump inside.
Then every child in the world will
have an Earth Spirit in their heart.
Then do you see what will happen?"
She said, "Then *they,* the children,
the People of tomorrow, will become

the guardians of the earth!"
"That's right," smiled Quill,
"That's why we're going to start playing
in the city dumps and in the bad places.
That's why we have to hurry.
We have to reach those
people who don't care.
We have to reach the children of the people
who can change the world.
You're going to walk in moccasins
across this land. You're going to
tell the whole wide world
'THIS EARTH HAS A SPIRIT.'
You're going to open the hearts
of all the children, and
you're going to do it with the Old Song—
Earth Mother Song, and with the Flute.
That's the job you were
Chosen for. Now you can
do it, because now mankind . . .
Blacks and Browns, Yellow
and White, and the Redmen
as well have lost
the World—lost the beauty,
and not until they have
lost it will they
realize their responsibility to it.

"Do you understand, Old,
Old Flute Lady?" asked Quill.
"Yes," she said, and then,
"Quill, before you leave . . ."
He said, "I've got to hurry, I've
got a lot of things to do yet."
"I know, but Quill, one
question I want to ask you.
Will I see you again?"
Quill looked at her and he said,
"You'll see me again, Little Girl,
Old, Old Flute Lady.
You and I are going back down in
that hole one day, together.
Altim Elut is waiting.
Now, look, look over there. You see,
there come three children.
Those are the first ones.
Get praying, Old Flute Lady.
Get praying."
And

Quill was gone.

Old, Old Flute Lady raised her Flute
and began to Pray.
The children began to
come her way.
Then . . .
She heard a bird sing very loudly.

She Opened Her Eyes and there she was,
back under her ancient tree friend,
back in the beautiful valley of her childhood.
She jumped up and looked around.
   "I'm still Little Girl, it
      was all just a dream."
But there, on the ground, where she had
fallen to sleep, was a Pure White Flute.
Little Girl lifted the Flute to her lips.
and the music rose up like magic.

"Little Girl Old Flute Lady", walks
the Earth and opens the hearts of the people.
When you're out on
the hillside alone,
or sitting by a campfire,
or you're down by the sea
or by a river,
or looking at a beautiful green hill
or standing with someone you love
    under a great tree,
and you suddenly hear the sound,
. . . way off . . .
of the Flute,
. . . think of your Earth Mother,
    and remember . . .
    She has a spirit,
    just like you and
    just like me.
    So, let your heart open;
    Remember—The Earth Mother has a spirit.

QUANAB

Quanab knocked the ashes from his pipe and swallowed the last of his cold coffee.

The moon had risen and was throwing its light through the aspen leaves, casting strange shadows on the floor of the forest of Charm Springs.

We stirred up the camp fire, put a load of aspen on it and built another pot of coffee. We sat for a long time looking into the fire, watching it burn and then die away.

"Grandfather?" I said.

"You have a question, little boy?" he said with a grin.

"Two questions, Grandfather. First, remember when Old Flute Lady and Quill were climbing the mound of trash in the city dump."

"Yes," he said, "you want to know about the book she found, don't you?"

"Yes," I answered, "how did you know?"

"Because you are supposed to want to know about that book," he said.

"Was it important?" I asked, "and what was the book about?"

"It was very important, that's why she found it, and that's why Quill told her to keep it," he said.

"What was it about, Grandfather?"

"Well," he said, "it was very important, and now it is very late; time to go to bed. What was your other question?"

"Well . . ." I said, "have you ever seen a Pockwatchie or a Tlaloque?"

"I see them every day," he answered. "That's why I live here on Spirit Mountain, among the aspens and pines. That's why I drink spring water and eat wild foods. And, little boy, who do you think told me the story of the Praying Flute?"

"Pockwatchies?"

He smiled and told me to go to bed.

Just before I went to sleep, I asked him once more about the book.

"What was the book about, Grandfather?"

"The book," he said, "that very important book she found in the dump was about 'time.' "

"And that, little boy, is another story."

Night time at Charm Springs on Bald Mountain.

Good Night!

SONG OF THE EARTH MOTHER

Composed by Tony Shearer and scored by D.J. Nagle.

Do you remember when Little Girl was down in the cave with Altim Elut? Do you remember when he gave her the flute and told her the secret? The music above is the song of the Earth Mother. It was the music Little Girl played forever after. With this music you can learn the song yourself. Ask your teacher or parent to play it for you. It sounds beautiful on a piano, and is unforgettable on a five-hole Lakota flute.

ABOUT THE AUTHOR

In 1971 Naturegraph Publishers, Inc. presented my first book, *Lord of the Dawn, Quetzalcoatl,* the story of the Plumed Serpent, a Toltic Priest King of Ancient Mexico. That book also told of the prophecies of the Thirteen Heavens and Nine Hells of the Sacred Calendar, and prophesied the end of the Fifth Sun, August 16, 1987. Now, fifteen years later, while *Lord of the Dawn* is still in print, Naturegraph presents *Praying Flute, Song of the Earth Mother.* I am honored that this has happened. And I thank you, my readers, because without your enthusiasm my dreams and visions that this would happen may never have been realized.

Now I am sixty years old and I gaze at my own five hole Lakota Flute and the two little books I have delivered from my life, and I say, "Thank you Great Spirit." Thank you for all my blessings, because with my flute and my stories I have travelled the Earth as a messenger from our dear and glorious Earth Mother. I have touched the hearts of thousands of children in nearly every land in the world, and prayed the Song of the Earth Mother in almost every country in the world. It has been my privilege, and I have realized the reality of a vision set forth twenty years ago when I laid aside my security and set out to accomplish a mission. That mission was to become a champion for Native American People (Indian and Chicano) and to become a guardian for my Earth Mother, a Warrior of the Rainbow.

"Mission Accomplished."

Now, one book remains to be written. It is the last book to complete my "Earth Mother Trilogy." I have waited twenty years in order to collect the material needed to make it a unique experience for my readers, and an unforgettable statement about the myths and legends of the Americas. The last book is called *The Boy and the Tree,* and with the continued blessings of the Great Spirit, it will be completed by August 16, 1987 . . . . .

Thank you.

The *Praying Flute* on cassette! Order below.

The Praying Flute
"Song of the Earth Mother"

Now on audio cassette! Recorded with state of the arts equipment at the University of New Mexico in Albuquerque, it features Tony Shearer as Quanab, the old story teller. Jeff Johnson is Little Boy, Kaare Evensen Jr. and his son Chris are the traditional Native American singers and drummers, and Victory Arenson is the feminine voice.

The experience was created for classroom use as well as for meditative listening. You will also find the cassette a perfect companion to the book. This cassette is not offered through any retail outlet.

Send $10.00 and your name and address to:
Amon Olorin
Route 1,   Box 2060
Arlee, MT   59821

Make check or money order payable to **Penny Light.**

Note: We ask that you do not copy the tape as a respect to the artist. Thank you.